AWESOME JOKES THAT EVERY 6 YEAR OLD SHOULD KNOW!

Names, characters, places, and products are used fictitiously. Any resemblance to actual persons, living or dead, events, or locales is entirely coincidental. If you're reading this and you're six, I'm very impressed.

Depending on where you live, some spellings might seem odd to you like colour, or favourite. I've done it on purpose: I'm aktually quite good at spelling. OK, it's because I'm from England and I'm no good at baseball jokes. Just skip over the ones you don't understand, and I hope you enjoy the others!

Additional research: Olivera Ristovska

Design: Fanni Williams / thehappycolourstudio.com
Icons: Freepik, Smashicons & mynamepong from www.flaticon.com

www.matwaugh.co.uk

Produced by Big Red Button Books,
a division of Say So Media Ltd.

ISBN: 978-1-9999147-2-1

Published: April 2018
This edition: July 2019

AWESOME JOKES THAT EVERY 6 YEAR OLD SHOULD KNOW!

MAT WAUGH
ILLUSTRATIONS BY YURKO RYMAR

Introduction

What is funny?

Is it when your brother gets stuck in the mud? I think that's quite funny.

Is it when milk spurts out of your nose? I think that's very funny.

Or is it anything that gives you a happy feeling? Stuff that makes you laugh so hard that your tummy hurts and your eyes do a little wee?

I hope you find jokes like that in this book. They're my very best jokes for 6 year olds.

That's an egg-cellent start!

Let's Get Cracking!

Why couldn't the boy get to sleep at his Grandma's house?

Because it was a lighthouse!

What kind of key opens a banana?

A monkey!

I feel like a dog, what should I do?
Sit!

What did the dog say when he unwrapped his Christmas bone?
That's the pawfect present!

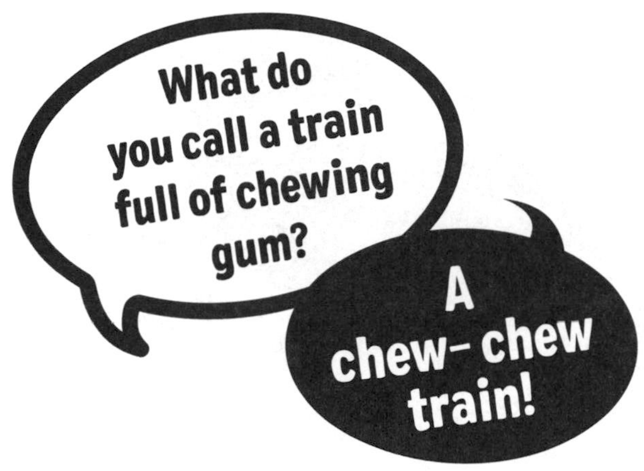

How do you stop Eskimos fighting?
Tell them to cool it!

What are the hottest days of summer?
Sun-days!

Why was the girl sitting on her clock?
Because she wanted to be on time!

What's orange and sounds like a parrot?
A carrot!

What do you call a fairy that doesn't like to wash?
Stinkerbell!

Why did the egg go to the doctor?
Because he had a cracking headache!

(Shout the answer to this one out loud!)

What is a pirate's favourite letter?

Aaarrrgh!

Knock Knock!

Who's there?

Witches.

Witches who?

Witches the way home?

What do you call a man lying on your doorstep?
Mat!
(Hey, is this joke being rude about me?)

What do kittens like to eat?
Mice cream!

How do you spell mousetrap with just three letters?
C-A-T.

How do ghosts clean their hair?
With sham-BOO!

What flies around the school buildings at night?

The alpha-bat!

What do blue whales eat?

Fish and ships!

What falls down but never gets hurt?

Rain!

What kind of apple isn't an apple?
A pineapple!

What has four legs and can't walk?
A table.
(It's not very funny but it's true!)

Knock Knock!

Who's there?

Ice cream.

Ice cream who?

Ice cream if you don't let me in!

What kind of beans won't grow in the garden?

Jelly beans!

What do you call a sleeping dinosaur?

A dino-snore!

Why do fish live in salty water?
Because pepper water makes them sneeze!

What do elves learn in school?
The elf-abet.

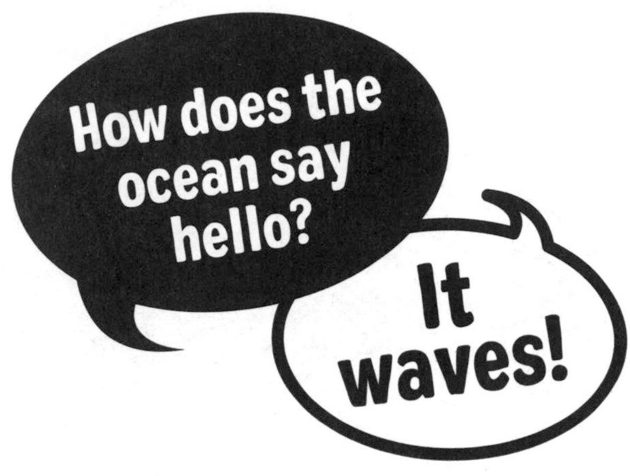

How do you make a milk shake?
Creep up behind it and shout BOO!

Why did the cookie go to the doctor?
He was feeling crummy!

What do cows listen to?

Moo-sic!

(Did you guess that one?)

Here's a tricky one to say quickly!

Round and round the rugged rock the ragged rascal ran.

What do you call a fly without wings?
A walk!

What happened when the tiger ate the clown?
He felt funny!

Knock Knock!

Who's there?

I am!

I am who?

Don't you even know who you are? Silly billy!

What do you call two birds in love?

Tweethearts!

What kind of key opens the door at Christmas?
A turkey!

What type of music scares balloons?
Pop music!

Knock Knock!

Who's there?
Harry.
Harry who?
Harry up, it's freezing out here!

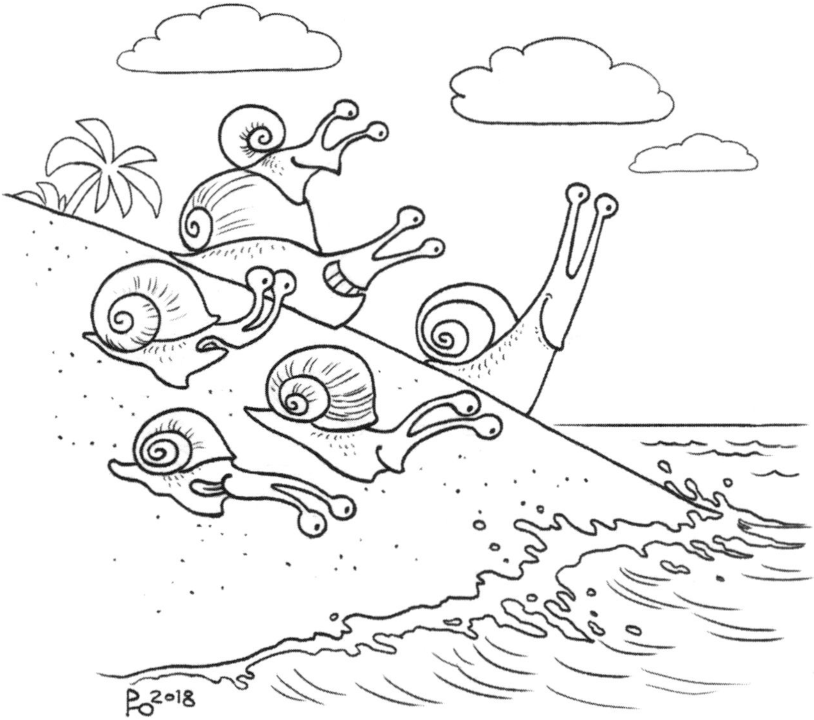

Can you say this 10 times quickly?

Six slippery snails slid slowly seaward.

What do you call shoes made from bananas?

Slippers!

(Do you know anyone with knobbly knees like this?!)

How does a farmer unlock his front door?

With a don-key!

How do bees get to school?
They take the school buzz!

What kind of fish is famous?
A star fish!

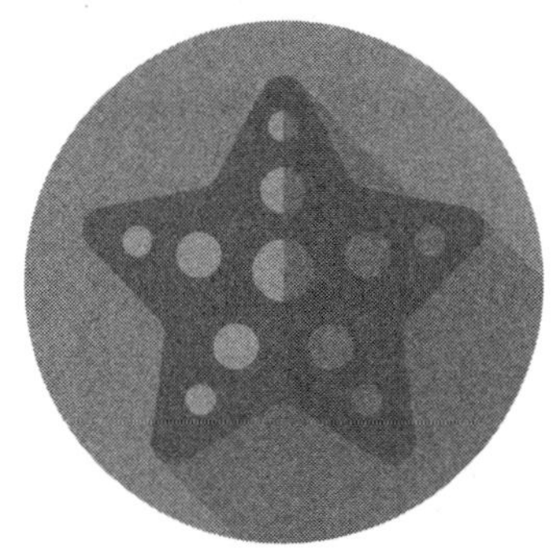

Knock Knock!

Who's there?
Smell mop.
Smell mop who?
You're disgusting. I don't want to smell your poo!

DOCTOR, DOCTOR!

I think I'm turning into a bee!
Buzz off – can't you see I'm busy?
(How rude!)

What did the peanut say to the monkey?
Nothing, of course. Peanuts don't talk.

Why did the farmer tiptoe around the farm?

He didn't want to wake the bull-dozer!

How do you catch a squirrel?

Climb a tree and act nuts!

What colour is a burp?

Burple!

Do you know what the triangle is in the picture? It's a prism – it splits white light into all the different colours (including purple!), just like a rainbow.

Will the pancakes be long?

No sir, they'll be round.

What's an astronaut's favourite chocolate?

A Mars bar!

What did the bus driver say to the frog?

Hop on!

What do witches put on their hair?
Scare spray!

Where do you find a birthday present for your kitten?
In a cat-alog!

There's a fly in the butter!
Yes sir, it's a butterfly!

How did the frog feel when he broke his leg?

Very unhoppy.

Knock Knock!

Who's there?

Sorry!

Sorry who?

Sorry, I've forgotten the end of this joke.

Who delivers Christmas presents to cats?

Santa Claws!

What's a ghost's favourite dessert?

Boo-berry pie!

Why did the banana go to the hospital?
Because he wasn't peeling well!

What game do baby ghosts like to play?
Hide-and-shriek!

Knock Knock!

Who's there?

Isabel.

Isabel who?

Is the bell working? I had to knock!

Why was the cucumber mad?

Because it was in a pickle!

(I don't like pickles. Do you?)

Why do people go to bed?

Because the bed won't go to them!

What sound does a nut make when it sneezes?
Cashew!

Why did the balloon burst?
Because it saw a lolly pop.

Why did the melon jump in the pool?

It thought it was a water-melon.

What do you call a dream about crocodiles snapping at your bottom?

A bitemare!

This one looks easy, but it's not! Give it a go!
Can you can a can as a canner can can a can?

Who's there?
Leaf.
Leaf who?
Leaf me alone!

What game do tornadoes like to play?
Twister!
(Do you know how to play Twister? It's great fun!)

Who's there?
Boo.
Boo who?
Don't cry, it's only me!

What's this fly doing in my soup?
It looks like it's learning to swim sir!

Who never gets invited to picnics but comes anyway?

Wasps!

What do snakes use to cut paper?

Scissss-ors!

How does a mouse feel after a bath?

Squeaky clean!

(This is my favourite pic by Yurko, who did all the fabulous line drawings. Which do you like?)

Knock Knock!

Who's there?

Some bunny.

Some bunny who?

Some bunny has been eating all my carrots!

How do you make toast in the jungle?
Put it under a grilla.
(Sorry, that's a terrible joke!)

Knock Knock!

Who's there?
Amos.
Amos who?
A mosquito bit me!
(That's another awful stinker!)

Why does a duck say quack?
Because it can't say moo.
(The jokes on this page really suck!)

Here's one to ask your mum or dad!

Did you hear about the grown-up with cabbage breath who keeps saying 'No'?

If they say no, they have cabbage breath - see if they fall for it!

Why did six run away?

Because 7 ate 9!

Where does Santa stay when he is on holiday?

In a ho-ho-hotel!

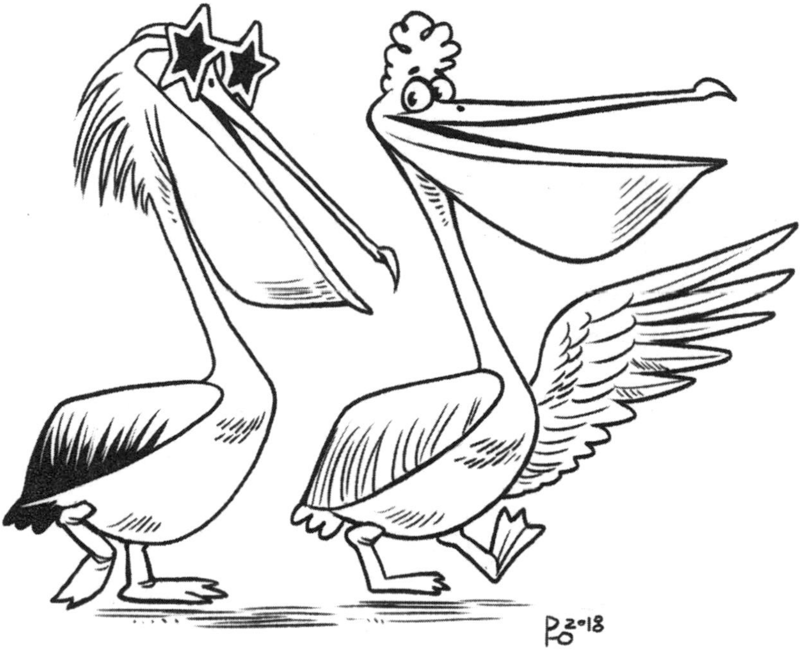

Try saying this one 7 times without a mistake!

Pooped purple pelicans plodding to a party.

What's the best thing to put in a pie?

Your teeth!

What happens when a frog breaks down?

He gets toad away!

What's the biggest net in the universe?
A pla-net!

What do giraffes tell each other?
Tall stories!

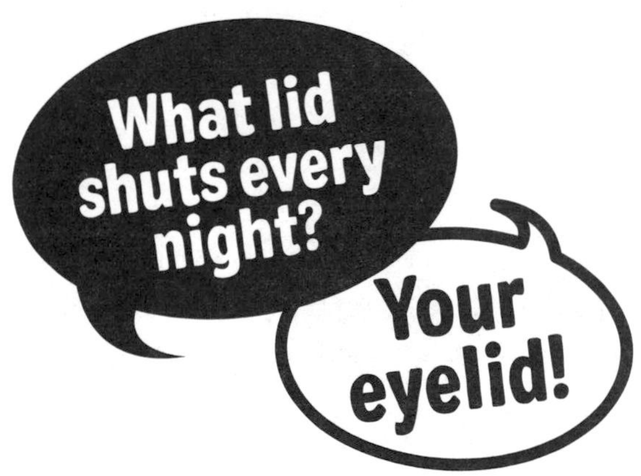

How do chickens dance at the Christmas party?
Chick to chick!

Why is a bamboo cane the scariest thing in the garden?
Because when the cane goes 'bam', you go BOO!
(Do you even get this joke? I'm not sure I do!)

I feel like a pair of curtains.
Oh, pull yourself together!

Why did the cow cross the road?
To get to the udder side.
(This joke is so old the dinosaurs probably invented it!)

How do you close an envelope in the ocean?
With a seal!

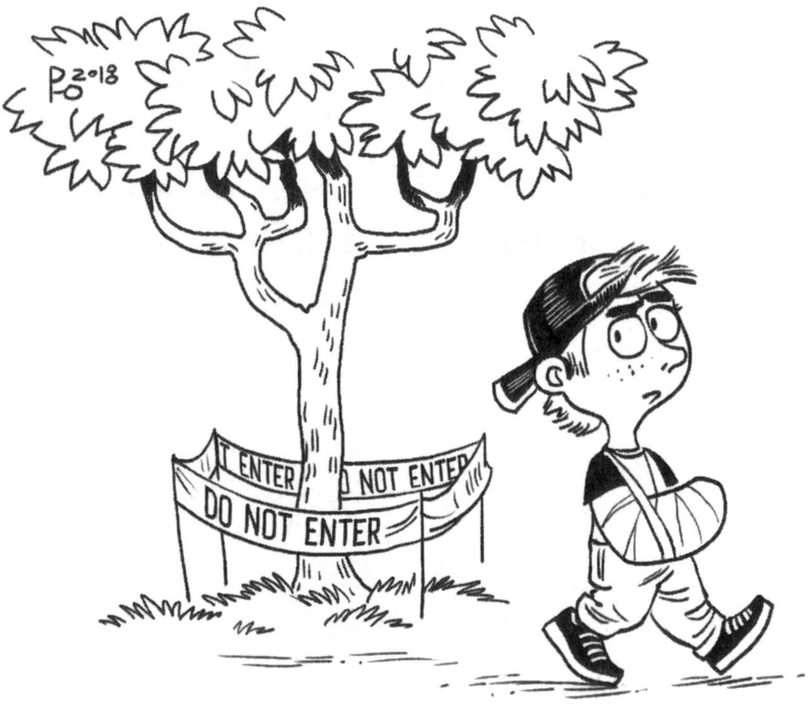

I've broken my arm in two places. What should I do?

Don't go to either of those places again!

This soup tastes funny.
So why aren't you laughing?

Who's there?
Tank.
Tank who?
You're welcome!

Get those lips ready!
Swan swam over the sea, swim, swan, swim! Swan swam back again. Well swum, swan!

Who's there?
Yah!
Yah who?
Ride 'em cowboy!

What is a maths teacher's favourite season?
Summer!

Knock Knock!

Who's there?
Annie.
Annie who?
Is Annie-body home?

What do you call a baby insect?
A baby buggy!

Why did Harry take a ruler to bed?
Because he wanted to see how long he slept!

How do fireflies start a race?
Ready, steady, glow!

My son has swallowed a pen! What should I do?
Why don't you use a pencil instead?

What is a bear's favourite drink?
Coca-Koala!

Why has a giraffe got a long neck?
Because his feet stink.

Knock Knock!

Who's there?

Icing.

Icing who?

Icing so loud, the neighbours are complaining!

What did the sheep say after he trod on the pig's toe?
Paaaaaardon me.

What do you get when you cross a dinosaur and fireworks?
Dino-mite!

Why do penguins never come to parties?
Because they always get cold feet.

Knock Knock!

Who's there?
Twig.
Twig who?
Twig or tweet!

What do you call a teacher wearing earmuffs?

Anything you like – he can't hear you!

What do you call a greedy elf?
Elfish!

What is the difference between a fly and a bird?
A bird can fly but a fly can't bird!

Why do humming birds hum?
Because they don't know the words!

What is the biggest ant in the world?
An elephant.

Now it's your turn!

Here are a few awesome jokes sent in by 6-year-olds from around the world. Do you know any funny jokes?

What do you get if you blow warm air down a rabbit hole?
Hot cross bunnies!
(From Holly, Deal)

Knock Knock!
Who's there?
Candle.
Candle who?
Why did you say my name!
(From Lucya, High Brooms – and no, I'm not sure I get that one either!)

Sent in by Iris, aged 6, from Lincoln

Why do gorillas have big nostrils?

Because they have big fingers!

Mix and match!

Can you match each joke to its punchline? But watch out: there are two questions missing! You'll find them in **More Awesome Jokes Every 6 Year Old Should Know** – out now!

What do you call a boy with his tongue out?

What did one butcher say to the other?

Why was the flight so bumpy?

Which prison bars get smaller the more they're used?

What do you call a pixie in a wig?

Which farm animal can open a door?

Which card games do crocodiles play?

Bars of soap!

It was a flight of steps!

That's not a worm, sir, it's just a lively piece of spaghetti.

A battering ram!

A hairy fairy!

Pleased to meat you!

SNAP!

Yippee – it's all ewe can eat!

Rudy!

How funny was that?

If you or your child enjoyed the jokes in this book, I'm really pleased! (If not, please write your complaint on a fifty pound note and send to my address straight away).

If you're feeling kind, there's something really important you can do for me – rate this book on Amazon.

If you do write something nice, let me know – I promise I'll write back. My email address for jokes, notes and more is jokes@matwaugh.co.uk

A gecko's eyesight is 350 times better than a human. Are you a gecko?

I know a great joke!

Send me your best joke and I'll put it on my **World Map of Awesome Jokes**!

Head over to the map now to discover silly jokes, clever jokes and weird jokes. Some jokes rhyme, some are a crime, but they're all sent in by children like you!

Will you be the first on the map from your town?

Put your awesome joke here at
www.matwaugh.co.uk/jokemap

About Mat Waugh

It's funny what makes you laugh, isn't it? Sometimes it's a great joke, and I hope you found a few in this book. Sometimes you don't even need words. It could be a funny look from a friend. Or maybe it's something that wasn't supposed to happen.

Once, when I was about six, I was in the back of my aunt's car on a Christmas Day. The sun reflected brightly in the deep puddles from the night's rain.

My aunt wasn't very good at driving. As we approached a dip in the road we could see a vicar cycling towards us, on his way to church. Dad told my aunt to slow down... but she pressed the wrong pedal. The car hit the water with a mighty SPLOOSH! I looked back to see a huge wave swamping the vicar and his bike. He shook his fists at us, but my aunt didn't even notice. I'm still laughing... but I bet the vicar isn't.

I have three daughters to make me laugh now. (Not all the time though: they drive me bananas.)

I live in Tunbridge Wells, which is a lively, lovely town in the south east of England. It's not a very funny place, mind you....

I've always written a lot. I've done lots of writing for other people – mostly serious stuff – but now I write silly, crazy and funny books as well.

Talking of crazy, I had a mad year when I thought I wanted to be a teacher. But then I found out how hard teachers work and that you have to buy your own biscuits. So now I just visit schools to eat their snacks and talk to children about stories.

Last thing: I love hearing from readers. Thoughts, jokes... anything. If that's you, then get in touch.

mail@matwaugh.co.uk
www.matwaugh.co.uk

Or, if you're old enough:

facebook.com/matwaughauthor
twitter.com/matwaugh

Three more to try!

Cheeky Charlie vol 1–6

Meet Harriet and her small, stinky brother. Together, they're trouble. Fabulously funny stories for kids aged 6 and up.

Fantastic Wordsearches

Wordsearch with a difference: themed, crossword clues and hidden words await!

What's the Magic Word?

It's Alfie's birthday, but it's not going to plan! If only he could remember the magic word - can you help him? For forgetful children aged 4+.

Available from Amazon and local bookshops.

Be the first to know about new stuff! Sign up for my emails at matwaugh.co.uk

What Dos a cow lisin to mousic!

Wath
Fall Daw
But Dose
Not ge
hrat Tain